D1808120

GCSE English Literature AQA (A)

This workbook covers all aspects of the AQA English Literature Specification A written paper. The purpose of this paper is to test your skills in the following areas:

- reading response to post-1914 prose texts
- reading response to pre-and post-1914 poetry

The examination paper will be divided into two sections. You have to answer one question from each section.

- **Section A (post-1914 prose).** You have to answer one question, from a choice of two, on one of the set novels or two short stories from the *AQA Anthology* (45 minutes).
- **Section B (pre-1914 and post-1914 poetry).** You have to compare one poem by each of your chosen pair of poets (**Heaney and Clarke** *or* **Duffy and Armitage**) with two poems from the **Pre-1914 Poetry Bank** in the *AQA Anthology* (1 hour).

To succeed in GCSE English Literature you need to read and understand your set texts and write clearly about them. When you read a work of literature you must try to grasp what the writer intended to convey to the reader. This can mean looking at the wider message that a book contains or exploring the different meanings a line of poetry might have. Throughout this workbook you will find examples and advice on how to do this.

Over the 2 years of your course you will look at many different forms of question and will study your set texts carefully. The final stage in your preparation is to organise your ideas into clear patterns so that you are ready to tackle the questions that come up in the exam. The advice and exercises in this workbook will help you to do this.

The ladder of skills

Your examination answers will be marked using a document called a mark scheme. It is probably more helpful for you to think of the ideas in the mark scheme as a ladder of skills, as shown.

Improving your grade in English Literature involves moving up the ladder of skills. You need to see that some skills are worth more than others and bear this in mind when you are preparing for the examination.

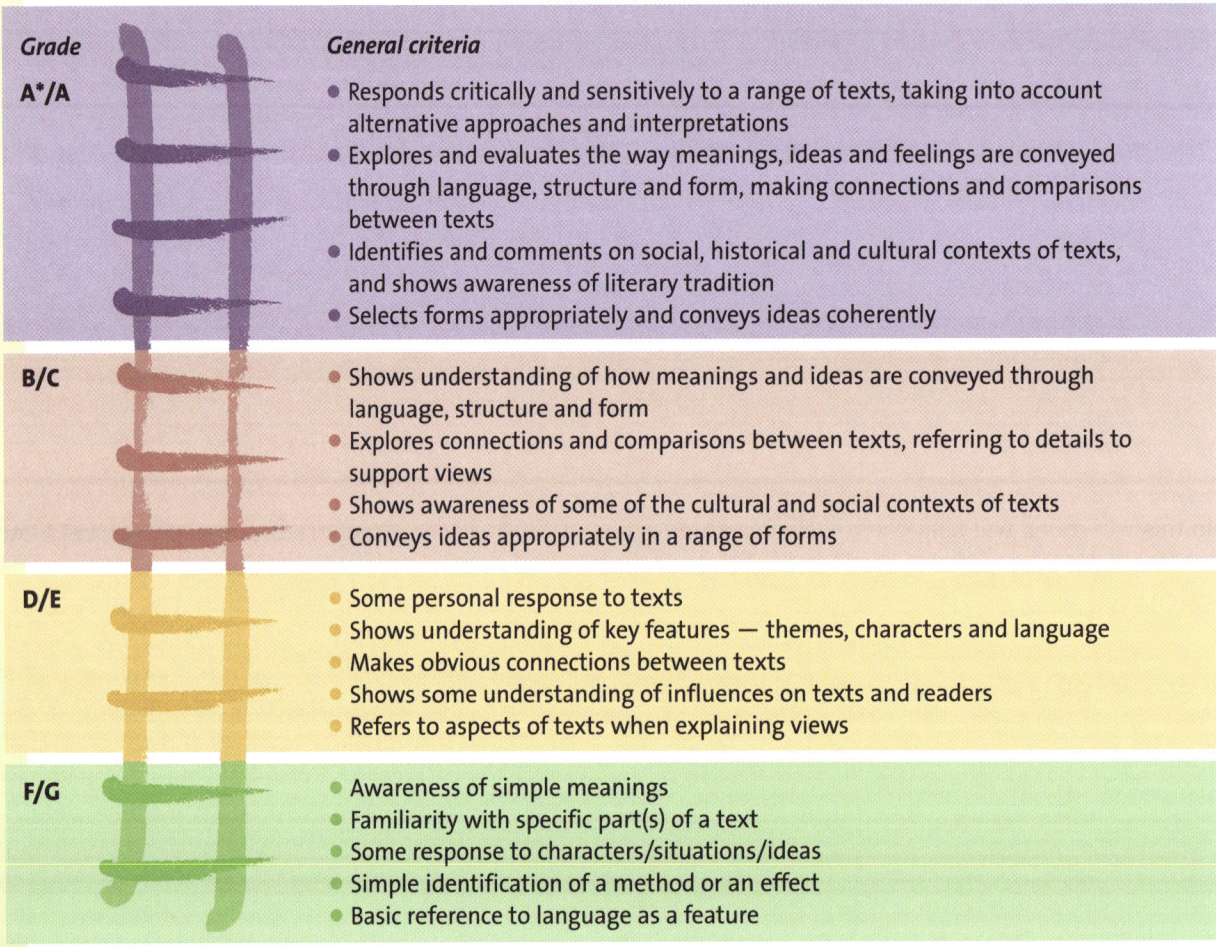

Grade	General criteria
A*/A	• Responds critically and sensitively to a range of texts, taking into account alternative approaches and interpretations • Explores and evaluates the way meanings, ideas and feelings are conveyed through language, structure and form, making connections and comparisons between texts • Identifies and comments on social, historical and cultural contexts of texts, and shows awareness of literary tradition • Selects forms appropriately and conveys ideas coherently
B/C	• Shows understanding of how meanings and ideas are conveyed through language, structure and form • Explores connections and comparisons between texts, referring to details to support views • Shows awareness of some of the cultural and social contexts of texts • Conveys ideas appropriately in a range of forms
D/E	• Some personal response to texts • Shows understanding of key features — themes, characters and language • Makes obvious connections between texts • Shows some understanding of influences on texts and readers • Refers to aspects of texts when explaining views
F/G	• Awareness of simple meanings • Familiarity with specific part(s) of a text • Some response to characters/situations/ideas • Simple identification of a method or an effect • Basic reference to language as a feature

Essay writing

The word 'essay' means 'an attempt' and is usually one person's thoughts on a given subject. In your English Literature examination you will be writing essays about novels or short stories and poetry. No matter what your essay is about, there are some general rules that you can follow. These are outlined in the box below.

A typical essay will usually contain:
- **an introduction** — where you suggest what you are going to say
- **the main body of the essay** — where you say it
- **a conclusion** — where you sum up what you have said

Essay writing is a skill that requires practice. The exercises in this workbook will help you to develop your essay-writing skills in preparation for your English Literature exam.

Assessment objectives

Your essays will be assessed against the objectives outlined below.

You must demonstrate your ability to:
- respond to texts **critically, sensitively and in detail**, selecting suitable ways to convey your response, using **textual evidence** as appropriate
- explore how **language, structure and forms** contribute to the meaning of texts, considering different approaches to texts and alternative interpretations
- explore **relationships and comparisons** within and between texts, selecting and evaluating relevant material
- show your understanding of literary tradition and appreciation of **social and historical influences and cultural contexts**

Section A Prose

By the end of year 11 you should have read your chosen text thoroughly **at least three times**. There is no substitute for knowing your way around the text.

For the 2004 examination only, students will be allowed to take annotated copies of set texts into the examination. From 2005 onwards, students' copies of set texts must not be annotated.

Before you take the exam you should:

- Know where key passages concerning each character or event can be found. This might be the page on which a character makes a first appearance or the point at which he/she is involved in an important incident. Practise making lists of such pages so that the information sticks in your head.
- Map out the plot of the novel/short story yourself so that you know exactly the sequence of events. Getting the order of major events wrong is not going to impress an examiner.

- Practise writing short answers. This way you will build up a library of comments that you know are successful. You should not be experimenting with new ideas in the exam.
- Build up a vocabulary of useful words and phrases that will help you to compare and contrast elements of the texts. You could practise using the following words and phrases:
  — on the other hand
  — whereas
  — although
  — however
  — though it might seem that...
  — while the author clearly attempts...

Words and phrases such as these make the examiner aware that you are thinking about the text and are not simply attempting to write it out in your own words.

Writing essays on prose texts

A typical essay on a prose text will contain comments on many aspects of the text. You will have to decide on the actual requirements based on the individual question, but you should be prepared to write about:

- plot (related to the question)
- character
- setting
- dialogue
- language
- purpose
- effectiveness
- mood
- point of view

Know your way around the text

In order to be able to write a good essay in the 45 minutes that you have available in the exam, it is vital that you know your way around the text. You cannot afford to spend a long time trying to find a particular incident or quotation.

Look at the key words in the question

This workbook is full of questions. Each of these questions has certain key words which need to be followed carefully. Take the following example:

How does Dickens **establish the character** of Fagin **without telling** the reader directly about him?

The key words in this question have been highlighted. You should practise highlighting the key words in questions that you face. A good way to get started on this is to highlight the key words in every new question that you meet in this workbook.

1 Write down the key events in your set book in the order in which they happen.

Context

One of the key points to remember when writing about a piece of literature is to discuss the work with a sense of its original context. This means that you have to know something of the world in which the novel/short story was originally written and published.

Be prepared to write about the background, context and setting of your prose text. The phrase to remember is **social, cultural and historical perspective** (see the assessment objectives on page 3).

Although you have to do this, do not treat the English Literature exam as though it were history. For example:

> Knowing what *Animal Farm* was based on is helpful, *but* it is not directly about the Russian Revolution. Do not spend your time writing out the history of the Russian Revolution.

2 How does the social and historical context of your set text affect the way a modern reader approaches reading the text today?

Purpose and audience

A key element of any essay on a literary text is your comment on the writer's purpose and intended audience. You need to ask yourself the following questions about each text you study:

- Why did the writer write *this*?
- What is the motivation behind the piece?
- Who was the intended audience?
- Has the writer been successful?

Be prepared to let the examiner know that you are doing this by using the words **purpose, audience** and **writer/author** in your answer.

3 Write a brief summary of what the writer set out to do in your set text.

3 ....

....

....

....

....

....

....

....

Comparing and contrasting

Many questions require you to be able to compare and contrast different elements of your set text. This could take the form of:

- comparing two characters
- analysing different characters' reactions to the same event
- examining the opening and the closing of the book/short story

Look at the following examples of comparing words:

- whereas
- however
- although
- on the other hand
- alternatively

4 Can you think of any more comparing words or phrases?

4 ....

....

Characters

Questions

Answer the following questions with reference to your set text.

1 Write a few sentences about each of the major characters in your set text.

Examiner's tip

You might have to adapt these questions slightly to fit your text, e.g. there might be only one character in a certain part of your text, but the question might ask you about more than one character.

Questions often require you to write about the main characters in your chosen set text. Remember to focus on the requirements of the question — do not simply repeat all you know about a particular character. If you are asked about a character's role in one part of the text, you can refer to other parts, but only if relevant.

1

2 How do the two major characters react to the most important event in the text?

3 Explain how the author creates sympathy for the main character at an important stage of the story.

3

4 How does the speech of any two characters reveal aspects of their natures to the reader?

4

5 Some characters are good and some can seem evil. Write about two contrasting characters from your set text.

5

6 How do the actions of some of the characters shape the plot of the text?

7 Writers sometimes use humour to lighten the mood in a text. Give an account of one such incident in your set book.

Key incidents in the plot

The text that you have studied has been carefully constructed by the author. The order in which the incidents occur is not accidental, nor is it real.

It is often vital to the whole plot that events happen in a certain order. Take the simple example of a murder story:

- murder happens
- detective arrives
- suspects are interviewed
- crime is solved

On page 5 you were asked to write out the main events that take place in your set text in order. The questions in this section ask you to break the text down into:

- opening
- main body
- ending

Try to get used to thinking of the text as a series of incidents that has been constructed by the author for a purpose (see the advice on purpose and audience on page 7).

Questions

Answer the following questions with reference to your set text.

1 Select what you think is the main incident from the opening of the text. How does this incident link to later events?

1

2 Choose two major incidents from the central section of the text. What effect does each incident have on:

a the characters involved?

b the development of the plot as a whole?

2a

b

3 Think about the incident that defines the end of the novel. Trace the events that led to this particular incident.

4 Some incidents are clearly designed to provoke a response from the reader. Choose two such incidents and discuss how the reader is affected by them and why.

4

Central issues

Questions

Answer the following questions with reference to your set text.

1 What do you consider to be the central issue of the text? Discuss in detail the way that the author deals with this issue. What have you learned about it from your reading of the text?

A piece of literature is more than a story. You need to look at the way the author has chosen to present:

- issues (e.g. injustice)
- problems
- aspects of human nature
- the culture and society of the time

Your set book will have at least one such element. You need to be familiar with writing about these key points.

1

2 Pieces of literature usually contain a problem of some kind. Discuss the problems faced by the characters in the text. What do you learn about the characters from the way they react?

3 Discuss the ways that the text can be said to reveal something wider about human nature.

4 In what ways is the text:

a a product of its time and culture?

b an illustration of its time and culture?

4a

b

Prose extracts

In the examination you will have to write about your prose set text. The skills required in order to do this well can be developed using this section of the workbook. The passages that follow are taken deliberately from texts that do not appear on the list of set books. The exercises will lead you through the various skills that you need to practise for the examination.

Item 1 *Oliver Twist* by Charles Dickens

The walls and ceiling of the room were perfectly black with age and dirt. There was a deal table before the fire, upon which were a candle, stuck in a ginger-beer bottle, two or three pewter pots, a loaf and butter, and a plate. In a frying-pan, which was on the fire, and which was secured to the mantelshelf by a string, some sausages were cooking; and standing over them, with a toasting-fork in his hand, was a very old shrivelled Jew, whose villanous-looking and repulsive face was obscured by a quantity of matted red hair. He was dressed in a greasy flannel gown, with his throat bare; and seemed to be dividing his attention between the frying-pan and a clothes-horse, over which a great number of silk handkerchiefs were hanging. Several rough beds made of old sacks, were huddled side by side on the floor. Seated round the table were four or five boys, none older than the Dodger, smoking long clay pipes, and drinking spirits with the air of middle-aged men. These all crowded about their associate as he whispered a few words to the Jew; and then turned round and grinned at Oliver. So did the Jew himself, toasting-fork in hand.

'This is him, Fagin,' said Jack Dawkins; 'my friend Oliver Twist.'

The Jew grinned; and, making a low obeisance to Oliver, took him by the hand, and hoped he should have the honour of his intimate acquaintance. Upon this, the young gentlemen with the pipes came round him, and shook both his hands very hard — especially the one in which he held his little bundle. One young gentleman was very anxious to hang up his cap for him; and another was so obliging as to put his hands in his pockets, in order that, as he was very tired, he might not have the trouble of emptying them, himself, when he went to bed. These civilities would probably have been extended much farther, but for a liberal exercise of the Jew's toasting-fork on the heads and shoulders of the affectionate youths who offered them.

'We are very glad to see you, Oliver, very,' said the Jew. 'Dodger, take off the sausages; and draw a tub near the fire for Oliver. Ah, you're a-staring at the pocket-handkerchiefs! eh, my dear! There are a good many of 'em, ain't there? We've just looked 'em out, ready for the wash; that's all, Oliver; that's all. Ha! ha! ha!'

The latter part of this speech was hailed by a boisterous shout from all the hopeful pupils of the merry old gentleman. In the midst of which, they went to supper.

Oliver ate his share, and the Jew then mixed him a glass of hot gin and water: telling him he must drink it off directly, because another gentleman wanted the tumbler. Oliver did as he was desired. Immediately afterwards he felt himself gently lifted on to one of the sacks; and then he sank into a deep sleep.

Questions

Look carefully at the description of Fagin and answer the following questions.

1 List the elements of his appearance and actions.

2 Look closely at the colours in the room, what Fagin is holding and the way that he tricks Oliver with kindness. Which character is Fagin meant to resemble?

1

2

3 How does Dickens establish the character of Fagin without telling the reader directly about him?

3

Examiner's tip

Dickens expects the reader to make connections between the appearance of Fagin and well-known images. You should also note that Fagin is a Jew in an England that was deeply suspicious of anyone who was not Christian.

Item 2 *Far From the Madding Crowd* by Thomas Hardy

The field he was in this morning sloped to a ridge called Norcombe Hill. Through a spur of this hill ran the highway between Emminster and Chalk-Newton. Casually glancing over the hedge, Oak saw coming down the incline before him an ornamental spring waggon, painted yellow and gaily marked, drawn by two horses, a waggoner walking alongside bearing whip perpendicularly. The waggon was laden with household goods and window plants, and on the apex of the whole sat a woman, young and attractive. Gabriel had not beheld the sight for more than half a minute, when the vehicle was brought to a standstill just beneath his eyes.

'The tailboard of the waggon is gone, Miss,' said the waggoner.

'Then I heard it fall,' said the girl, in a soft, though not particularly low voice. 'I heard a noise I could not account for when we were coming up the hill.'

'I'll run back.'

'Do,' she answered.

The sensible horses stood perfectly still, and the waggoner's steps sank fainter and fainter in the distance.

The girl on the summit of the load sat motionless, surrounded by tables and chairs with their legs upwards, backed by an oak settle, and ornamented in front by pots of geraniums, myrtles and cactuses, together with a caged canary — all probably from the windows of the house just vacated. There was also a cat in a willow basket, from the partly-opened lid of which she gazed with half-closed eyes, and affectionately surveyed the small birds around.

The handsome girl waited for some time idly in her place, and the only sound heard in the stillness was the hopping of the canary up and down the perches of its prison. Then she looked attentively downwards. It was not at the bird, nor at the cat; it was at an oblong package tied in paper, and lying between them. She turned her head to learn if the waggoner were coming. He was not yet in sight; and her eyes crept back to the package, her thoughts seeming to run upon what was inside it. At length she drew the article into her lap, and untied the paper covering; a small swing looking-glass was disclosed, in which she proceeded to survey herself attentively. She parted her lips and smiled.

It was a fine morning, and the sun lighted up to a scarlet glow the crimson jacket she wore, and painted a soft lustre upon her bright face and dark hair. The myrtles, geraniums, and cactuses packed around her were fresh and green, and at such a leafless season they invested the whole concern of horses, waggon, furniture, and girl with a peculiar vernal charm. What possessed her to indulge in such a performance in the sight of the sparrows, blackbirds, and unperceived farmer who were alone its spectators — whether the smile began as a factitious one, to test her capacity in that art — nobody knows; it ended certainly in a real smile. She blushed at herself, and seeing her reflection blush, blushed the more...

... There was no necessity whatever for her looking in the glass. She did not adjust her hat, or pat her hair, or press a dimple into shape, or do one thing to signify that any such intention had been her motive in taking up the glass. She simply observed herself as a fair product of Nature in the feminine kind, her thoughts seeming to glide into far-off though likely dramas in which men would play a part — vistas of probable triumphs — the smiles being of a phase suggesting that hearts were imagined as lost and won. Still, this was but conjecture, and the whole series of actions was so idly put forth as to make it rash to assert that intention had any part in them at all.

The waggoner's steps were heard returning. She put the glass in the paper, and the whole again into its place.

When the waggon had passed on, Gabriel withdrew from his point of espial, and descending into the road, followed the vehicle to the turnpike-gate some way beyond the bottom of the hill, where the object of his contemplation now halted for the payment of toll. About twenty steps still remained between him and the gate, when he heard a dispute. It was a difference concerning twopence between the persons with the waggon and the man at the toll-bar.

'Mis'ess's niece is upon the top of the things, and she says that's enough that I've offered ye, you great miser, and she won't pay any more.' These were the waggoner's words.

'Very well; then mis'ess's niece can't pass,' said the turnpike-keeper, closing the gate.

Oak looked from one to the other of the disputants, and fell into a reverie. There was something in the tone of twopence remarkably insignificant. Threepence had a definite value as money — it was an appreciable infringement on a day's wages, and,

as such, a higgling matter: but twopence — 'Here,' he said, stepping forward and handing twopence to the gatekeeper; 'let the young woman pass.' He looked up at her then; she heard his words, and looked down.

Gabriel's features adhered throughout their form so exactly to the middle line between the beauty of St John and the ugliness of Judas Iscariot, as represented in a window of the church he attended, that not a single lineament could be selected and called worthy either of distinction or notoriety. The red-jacketed and dark-haired maiden seemed to think so too, for she carelessly glanced over him, and told her man to drive on. She might have looked her thanks to Gabriel on a minute scale, but she did not speak them; more probably she felt none, for in gaining her a passage he had lost her her point, and we know how women take a favour of that kind.

The gatekeeper surveyed the retreating vehicle. 'That's a handsome maid,' he said to Oak.

'But she has her faults,' said Gabriel.

'True, farmer.'

'And the greatest of them is well, what it is always.'

'Beating people down? ay, 'tis so.'

'O no.'

'What, then?'

Gabriel, perhaps a little piqued by the comely traveller's indifference, glanced to where he had witnessed her performance over the hedge, and said, 'Vanity.'

Question
·····································

What does the girl reveal about
herself through her actions in
this passage?

Examiner's tip

Look at the way she behaves
and how the two other
characters react to this.

Item 3 *Kidnapped* by Robert Louis Stevenson

Out I went into the night. The wind was still moaning in the distance, though never a breath of it came near the house of Shaws. It had fallen blacker than ever; and I was glad to feel along the wall, till I came the length of the stair-tower door at the far end of the unfinished wing. I had got the key into the keyhole and had just turned it, when all upon a sudden, without sound of wind or thunder, the whole sky lighted up with wild-fire and went black again. I had to put my hand over my eyes to get back to the colour of the darkness; and indeed I was already half blinded when I stepped into the tower.

It was so dark inside, it seemed a body could scarce breathe; but I pushed out with foot and hand, and presently struck the wall with the one, and the lowermost round of the stair with the other. The wall, by the touch, was of fine hewn stone; the steps too, though somewhat steep and narrow, were of polished masonwork, and regular and solid under foot. Minding my uncle's word about the banisters, I kept close to the tower side, and felt my way in the pitch darkness with a beating heart.

The house of Shaws stood some five full storeys high, not counting lofts. Well, as I advanced, it seemed to me the stair grew airier and a thought more lightsome; and I was wondering what might be the cause of this change, when a second blink of the summer lightning came and went. If I did not cry out, it was because fear had me by the throat; and if I did not fall, it was more by Heaven's mercy than my own strength. It was not only that the flash shone in on every side through breaches in the wall, so that I seemed to be clambering aloft upon an open scaffold, but the same passing brightness showed me the steps were of unequal length, and that one of my feet rested that moment within two inches of the well.

This was the grand stair! I thought; and with the thought, a gust of a kind of angry courage came into my heart. My uncle had sent me here, certainly to run great risks, perhaps to die. I swore I would settle that 'perhaps,' if I should break my neck for it; got me down upon my hands and knees; and as slowly as a snail, feeling before my every inch, and testing the solidity of every stone, I continued to ascend the stair. The darkness, by contrast with the flash, appeared to have redoubled; nor was that all, for my ears were now troubled and my mind confounded by a great stir of bats in the top part of the tower, and the foul beasts, flying downwards, sometimes beat about my face and body.

The tower, I should have said, was square; and in every corner the step was made of a great stone of a different shape, to join the flights. Well, I had come close to one of these turns, when, feeling forward as usual, my hand slipped upon an edge and found nothing but emptiness beyond it. The stair had been carried no higher: to set a stranger mounting it in the darkness was to send him straight to his death; and (although thanks to the lightning and my own precautions, I was safe enough) the mere thought of the peril in which I might have stood, and the dreadful height I might have fallen from, brought out the sweat upon my body and relaxed my joints.

How does Robert Louis Stevenson create atmosphere in this passage from *Kidnapped*?

Examiner's tip

Look closely at the description and the way it is used to create tension. You should also consider whether the author has put the reader ahead of the central character.

Item 4 *Tea* by Saki

James Cushat-Prinkly was a young man who had always had a settled conviction that one of these days he would marry; up to the age of thirty-four he had done nothing to justify that conviction. He liked and admired a great many women collectively and dispassionately without singling out one for especial matrimonial consideration, just as one might admire the Alps without feeling that one wanted any particular peak as one's own private property. His lack of initiative in this matter aroused a certain amount of impatience among the sentimentally minded women-folk of his home circle; his mother, his sisters, an aunt-in-residence, and two or three intimate matronly friends regarded his dilatory approach to the married state with a disapproval that was far from being inarticulate. His most innocent flirtations were watched with the straining eagerness which a group of unexercised terriers concentrates on the slightest movements of a human being who may be reasonably considered likely to take them for a walk. No decent-souled mortal can long resist the pleading of several pairs of walk-beseeching dog-eyes; James Cushat-Prinkly was not sufficiently obstinate or indifferent to home influences to disregard the obviously expressed wish of his family that he should become enamoured of some nice marriageable girl, and when his Uncle Jules departed this life and bequeathed him a comfortable little legacy it really seemed the correct thing to do to set about discovering some one to share it with him. The process of discovery was carried on more by the force of suggestion and the weight of public opinion than by any initiative of his own; a clear working majority of his female relatives and the aforesaid matronly friends had pitched on Joan Sebastable as the most suitable young woman in his range of acquaintance to whom he might propose marriage, and James became gradually accustomed to the idea that he and Joan would go together through the prescribed stages of congratulations, present-receiving, Norwegian or Mediterranean hotels, and eventual domesticity. It was necessary, however, to ask the lady what she thought about the matter; the family had so far conducted and directed the flirtation with ability and discretion, but the actual proposal would have to be an individual effort.

Cushat-Prinkly walked across the Park towards the Sebastable residence in a frame of mind that was moderately complacent. As the thing was going to be done he was glad to feel that he was going to get it settled and off his mind that afternoon. Proposing marriage, even to a nice girl like Joan, was a rather irksome business, but one could not have a honeymoon in Minorca and a subsequent life of married happiness without such preliminary. He wondered what Minorca was really like as a place to stop in; in his mind's eye it was an island in perpetual half-mourning, with black or white Minorca hens running all over it. Probably it would not be a bit like that when one came to examine it. People who had been in Russia had told him that they did not remember having seen any Muscovy ducks there, so it was possible that there would be no Minorca fowls on the island.

His Mediterranean musings were interrupted by the sound of a clock striking the half-hour. Half-past four. A frown of dissatisfaction settled on his face. He would arrive at the Sebastable mansion just at the hour of afternoon tea. Joan would be seated at a low table, spread with an array of silver kettles and cream-jugs and delicate porcelain teacups, behind which her voice would tinkle pleasantly in a series of little friendly questions about weak or strong tea, how much, if any, sugar, milk, cream, and so forth. 'Is it one lump? I forgot. You do take milk, don't you? Would you like some more hot water, if it's too strong?'

Cushat-Prinkly had read of such things in scores of novels, and hundreds of actual experiences had told him that they were true to life. Thousands of women, at this solemn afternoon hour, were sitting behind dainty porcelain and silver fittings, with their voices tinkling pleasantly in a cascade of solicitous little questions. Cushat-Prinkly detested the whole system of afternoon tea. According to his theory of life a woman should lie on a divan or couch, talking with incomparable charm or looking unutterable thoughts, or merely silent as a thing to be looked on, and from behind a silken curtain a small Nubian page should silently bring in a tray with cups and dainties, to be accepted silently, as a matter of course, without drawn-out chatter about cream and sugar and hot water. If one's soul was really enslaved at one's mistress's feet, how could one talk coherently about weakened tea? Cushat-Prinkly had never expounded his views on the subject to his mother; all her life she had been accustomed to tinkle pleasantly at tea-time behind dainty porcelain and silver, and if he had spoken to her about divans and Nubian pages she would have

urged him to take a week's holiday at the seaside. Now, as he passed through a tangle of small streets that led indirectly to the elegant Mayfair terrace for which he was bound, a horror at the idea of confronting Joan Sebastable at her tea-table seized on him. A momentary deliverance presented itself; on one floor of a narrow little house at the noisier end of Esquimault Street lived Rhoda Ellam, a sort of remote cousin, who made a living by creating hats out of costly materials. The hats really looked as if they had come from Paris; the cheques she got for them unfortunately never looked as if they were going to Paris. However, Rhoda appeared to find life amusing and to have a fairly good time in spite of her straitened circumstances. Cushat-Prinkly decided to climb up to her floor and defer by half-an-hour or so the important business which lay before him; by spinning out his visit he could contrive to reach the Sebastable mansion after the last vestiges of dainty porcelain had been cleared away.

Rhoda welcomed him into a room that seemed to do duty as workshop, sitting-room, and kitchen combined, and to be wonderfully clean and comfortable at the same time.

'I'm having a picnic meal,' she announced. 'There's caviare in that jar at your elbow. Begin on that brown bread-and-butter while I cut some more. Find yourself a cup; the teapot is behind you. Now tell me about hundreds of things.'

She made no other allusion to food, but talked amusingly and made her visitor talk amusingly too. At the same time she cut the bread-and-butter with a masterly skill and produced red pepper and sliced lemon, where so many women would merely have produced reasons and regrets for not having any. Cushat-Prinkly found that he was enjoying an excellent tea without having to answer as many questions about it as a Minister for Agriculture might be called on to reply to during an outbreak of cattle plague.

'And now tell me why you have come to see me,' said Rhoda suddenly. 'You arouse not merely my curiosity but my business instincts. I hope you've come about hats. I heard that you had come into a legacy the other day, and, of course, it struck me that it would be a beautiful and desirable thing for you to celebrate the event by buying brilliantly expensive hats for all your sisters. They may not have said anything about it, but I feel sure the same idea has occurred to them. Of course, with Goodwood on us, I am rather rushed just now, but in my business we're accustomed to that; we live in a series of rushes — like the infant Moses.'

'I didn't come about hats,' said her visitor. 'In fact, I don't think I really came about anything. I was passing and I just thought I'd look in and see you. Since I've been sitting talking to you, however, a rather important idea has occurred to me. If you'll forget Goodwood for a moment and listen to me, I'll tell you what it is.'

Some forty minutes later James Cushat-Prinkly returned to the bosom of his family, bearing an important piece of news.

'I'm engaged to be married,' he announced.

A rapturous outbreak of congratulation and self-applause broke out.

'Ah, we knew! We saw it coming! We foretold it weeks ago!'

'I'll bet you didn't,' said Cushat-Prinkly. 'If any one had told me at lunch-time today that I was going to ask Rhoda Ellam to marry me and that she was going to accept me, I would have laughed at the idea.'

The romantic suddenness of the affair in some measure compensated James's women-folk for the ruthless negation of all their patient effort and skilled diplomacy. It was rather trying to have to deflect their enthusiasm at a moment's notice from Joan Sebastable to Rhoda Ellam; but, after all, it was James's wife who was in question, and his tastes had some claim to be considered.

On a September afternoon of the same year, after the honeymoon in Minorca had ended, Cushat-Prinkly came into the drawing room of his new house in Granchester Square. Rhoda was seated at a low table, behind a service of dainty porcelain and gleaming silver. There was a pleasant tinkling note in her voice as she handed him a cup.

'You like it weaker than that, don't you? Shall I put some more hot water to it? No?'

Questions

1 How does the writer make James Cushat-Prinkly seem to be a rather silly man?

2 How does Saki ridicule the English tradition of afternoon tea?

Examiner's tip

Note that Saki does not attack anything directly but simply chooses to show how some behaviour is absurd.

1 ....

....

....

....

....

....

....

2 ....

....

....

....

....

....

....

3 Explain how the unexpected twist in the tale reveals the shallowness of the characters.

Quotations

One of the most important aspects of writing an English Literature essay is knowing how to use quotations to support your comments. You will have the text in front of you in the examination, so knowing the words themselves is not an issue. Where students fall down is in selecting inappropriate quotations or using far too much of the original text. The key to success in this is to **be selective**.

There are five basic principles to bear in mind when using quotations:

- put inverted commas at the beginning and end of the quotation
- write the quotation exactly as it appears in the original
- do not use a quotation that repeats what you have just written
- use the quotation so that it fits into your sentence
- keep the quotation as short as possible

Quotations should be used to develop your line of thought in your essays. Your comment should not duplicate what is in your quotation. For example:

> After the incident in the hotel, Holden says he felt miserable and depressed: 'Boy, I felt miserable. I felt so depressed, you can't imagine.'

It is far more effective to write:

> The incident in the hotel left Holden feeling '... miserable. I felt so depressed, you can't imagine.'

The most sophisticated way of using the writer's words is to embed them into your sentence. For example:

> In *Lord of the Flies* Jack's statement that 'I ought to be chief' reveals his arrogance.

When you use quotations in this way, you are demonstrating the ability to use text to support your ideas — not simply including words from the original to prove you have read it.

Questions

1 Using the passages on pages 23–33, select quotations that would be suitable for the following comments. You might have to add the odd connecting word yourself.

1a Dickens makes Fagin appear evil by describing him as ....

and showing him ....

b Oliver seems very innocent. When he thinks the other boys are helping him they are in fact ....

.... and .... in order to trick him into feeling at home with them.

c The reader can see that Bathsheba is vain when she ....

d Bathsheba knows she is rather childish when she ....

e In the passage from *Kidnapped* the uncle is cruel to his nephew. He sends him up the unfinished staircase

....

f Stevenson stresses the darkness of the staircase by saying it seemed so dark that ....

g The characters in *Tea* are obsessed with the trivial aspects of life, for example, ...

h Rhoda thinks that James Cushat-Prinkly has come to see her because ....

2 Now adapt the following general comments to suit the book you have studied.

2a The character of .... can be said to be ....

.... when he/she says ....

b The words .... reveal that ....

.... is ....

c The novel/short story entitled ....

can best be summed up by the line ....

.... from chapter ....

d The character of .... can be summed up with the words

....

Examiner's tip
Practise choosing quotations and keep a quotations book. This will get you used to thinking about selecting appropriate words and phrases to support your comments.

Section B Poetry

The poetry requirements for AQA GCSE English Literature Specification A are as follows:

- Study the poems by your chosen pair of poets in the *AQA Anthology* (your teacher will tell you which pair you need to study).
- Study the poems in the Pre-1914 Poetry Bank in the *AQA Anthology*.
- Find connections between the poems by your pair of poets and the poems in the Pre-1914 Poetry Bank.
- Write about **one poem** from **each** of your pair of poets and **two poems** from the Pre-1914 Poetry Bank.

Begin your preparation well in advance of your exam so that you are not thrown by the requirements of the poetry question in the exam.

Writing about poetry

Note the following points:

- poetry is a very condensed form of writing
- 'poetry is all about how you say a thing' (Robert Frost, an American poet)
- poetry is not 'funny writing' that needs to be translated
- the poet has made a series of choices — you must consider:
  — what these choices are
  — what effects these choices have on the reader

You need to have the correct vocabulary available to you in the examination. It is no good saying, 'I really like this poem. It was fun to read.' Such comments do not actually say anything. Be prepared to write clearly and to demonstrate that you have understood the poems you have read.

Collecting useful words and phrases is one way to go about this. Words and phrases which allow you to **compare** are especially useful. For example:

- The first poem deals with...whereas...
- The first poem deals with...as does...
- On the one hand...on the other hand...
- While...is about X the poem...is clearly discussing Y...

Question

Work out some of your own expressions for linking both similar and different poems.

Using themes to establish links

As you will be writing about a wide range of poems from at least three different poets and from different ages, you cannot be expected to answer a specific question linking particular poems. It is far more likely that you will be asked to address the themes that appear in a range of poems.

The themes might include:
- jealousy and resentment in relationships
- the way people are portrayed
- how one person's actions affect other people
- the manner in which people cope with difficult situations
- the way emotion is conveyed

Question

Use the table to group together poems that you know contain similar themes.

Theme	Post-1914 poems	Pre-1914 poems

Examiner's tip

Now that you have started to think about the themes that you need to explore, you have begun to think about the types of question that you will be asked in the examination.

Language

The aspect of the pre-1914 poems that you are likely to find most difficult is the language used. Language changes over time. The way that Shakespeare formed sentences is quite different from the way that you might do so today. Your teacher will help you to get to grips with the way that writers in this section of the *Anthology* use language.

Context

You can increase your understanding of the pre-1914 poems by finding out about the context in which they were written and/or set. For example, the two Robert Browning poems, 'My Last Duchess' and 'The Laboratory', both deal with insane jealousy and are in Gothic settings. They were written in the Victorian era and reflect the Victorians' love of all things Gothic. (Gothic literature is set in places such as draughty castles and includes the novel *Dracula*.)

However, it is important to note that **poems are not necessarily set when they were written**.

Question

Carry out your own research and then complete the following table for some of the other poems in the Pre-1914 Poetry Bank. One row has been completed for you as an example.

Poem	Setting	Date of publication	Context
'The Laboratory'	France in 15th or 16th century	1844	Victorians loved Gothic horror

Quotations

The same rules apply for choosing quotations from poetry as from prose (see page 36), but it is even more important that you select only the relevant words. Long quotations from poems are the sign of a weak candidate. It looks like you don't really know which words or lines you need, so you have copied out a large chunk of the poem to be on the safe side.

Always lay out the lines as they appear in the text. For example:

> 'Small round hard stones click
> under my heels'

The writer has decided where lines should end. You should not rewrite the text by changing the line endings, even if you can fit more words into a line of your writing.

Question

Select quotations from the poems in the Pre-1914 Poetry Bank that would be suitable for the following comments. You might have to add the odd connecting word yourself.

a   In 'Tichborne's Elegy' Charles Tichborne uses contrasts between his previous life and his current situation when he says .... and ....

b   In 'The Man He Killed' Hardy reveals that he feels the other soldier was just like him with the words ....
....

c   'In Sonnet 130' Shakespeare uses the well-known poetic device of comparing a woman to the beauties of nature. He says her .... are .... and her .... are

d   In 'My Last Duchess' the Duke calmly announces that he gave commands and that 'Then ....
....

e   In Robert Browning's 'The Laboratory' the poisons in the apothecary's shop are not described as being terrible and frightening but .... and ....

f   In Oliver Goldsmith's poem the village schoolmaster is obviously held in high regard by all around as people are amazed that ....

Questions on individual poems
Seamus Heaney

1 How does Heaney portray natural forces in 'Storm on the Island'?

1

2 Discuss the way the poet uses imagery to create effects in 'Perch'.

2

3 How does the poem 'Blackberry-Picking' convey the idea that nothing stays perfect forever?

4 In 'Death of a Naturalist' Heaney shows that nature can appear beautiful yet be quite threatening. Discuss the ways the poet brings out such ideas in the poem.

3

4

5 Comment on the different types of digging referred to in the poem 'Digging' and say what we learn from the poem about the speaker's relationships.

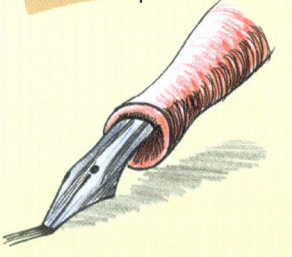

6 In the poem 'Mid-Term Break', how does Heaney convey the sorrow felt at the death of the speaker's younger brother?

5

6

7 Like 'Digging', the poem 'Follower' explores the speaker's relationship with his father. Comment on the way ideas are put across in this poem.

8 How is the relationship between people and the land explored in 'At a Potato Digging'?

7

8

Gillian Clarke

1 How does Clarke approach the subject of the mother–daughter relationship in 'Catrin' and 'Baby-Sitting'?

1

2 How does Clarke link the landscape to the birth of the child in 'Mali'?

3 How does Clarke show the close links between humans and nature in 'A Difficult Birth, Easter 1998'?

4 How does Clarke portray the idea that the world of man clashes with nature in 'The Field-Mouse'?

5 What does Clarke reveal about her feelings on ageing in 'October'?

4

5

6 What aspects of human behaviour does Clarke ridicule in 'On the Train'?

7 What elements of behaviour are discussed in 'Cold Knap Lake'?

Carol Ann Duffy

1 How does Duffy use language to portray hatred in 'Havisham'?

2 How has the character found peace by rejecting the material world in 'Elvis's Twin Sister'?

3 How does Duffy explore the theme of love in 'Anne Hathaway'?

4 What do you learn about the character's views of men from 'Salome'?

5 Examine the ways in which Duffy explores the speaker's relationship with her mother in 'Before You Were Mine'.

6 How does Duffy discuss the idea that adults see the world very differently from children in 'We Remember Your Childhood Well'?

7 Discuss the way Duffy reveals the breakdown of the character in 'Education for Leisure'.

8 How is the frustration of the central character brought out in 'Stealing'?

Simon Armitage

1 What do you learn of the character's feelings about his relationship with his mother in the lines from the poem 'Book of Matches' starting 'Mother...' (*AQA Anthology*, p. 39)?

2 How is the character influenced by his father in the lines from the poem 'Book of Matches' starting 'My father...' (*AQA Anthology*, p. 40)?

1

2

3 How is childhood linked to adult life in 'Homecoming'?

4 Discuss the way that ageing and death are explored in 'November'.

5 How does Armitage use childhood memories to comment on aspects of adult life in 'Kid'?

6 What ideas of social injustice are discussed in the poem 'Book of Matches' starting 'Those bastards...' (*AQA Anthology*, p. 44)?

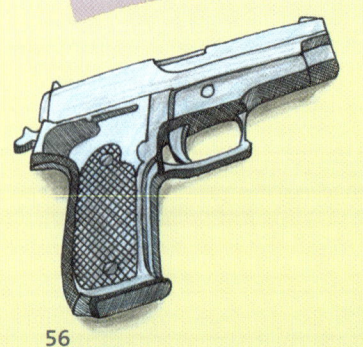

5

6

7 Comment on the poet's use of imagery to describe the speaker's attitude to death in the lines from the poem 'Book of Matches' starting 'I've made... (*AQA Anthology*, p. 44).

8 What is there in the life of the driver that makes him react in the way he does to the hitcher in 'Hitcher'?

7

8

Pre-1914 Poetry Bank

1 How does Jonson convey his sorrow in 'On my first Sonne'?

2 How does Yeats contrast the lives of mother and children in 'The Song of the Old Mother'?

1

2

3 Discuss the way Wordsworth gradually reveals the mother's sorrow in 'The Affliction of Margaret'.

4 Compare and contrast the idea of hope in 'The Little Boy Lost' and 'The Little Boy Found'.

AQA (A)

3

4

5 Discuss the way Tichbourne reveals his sadness and feelings of loss in 'Tichbourne's Elegy'.

6 How does Hardy explore the futility of war in 'The Man He Killed'?

5

6

7 Comment on the use of language to portray the savage weather in 'Patrolling Barnegat'.

8 In 'Sonnet 130', Shakespeare does not portray an ideal picture of a woman yet says she is still without compare. How does he turn insults into compliments in this poem?

7

8

9 'My Last Duchess' and 'The Laboratory' are both about insane jealousy. Discuss the methods Browning uses to reveal the state of mind of the narrator.

10 How does Tennyson use the epic form in 'Ulysses'?

11 Comment on the way Goldsmith conveys sympathy and affection for the schoolmaster in 'The Village Schoolmaster'.

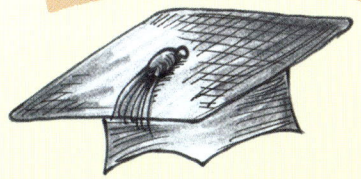

12 How do the poets convey their admiration for nature in 'The Eagle' and 'Inversnaid'?

11

12

13 Comment on Clare's use of imagery in 'Sonnet'.

13

Philip Allan Updates

Market Place, Deddington, Oxfordshire, OX15 0SE

Orders

Bookpoint Ltd, 130 Milton Park, Abingdon, Oxfordshire, OX14 4SB
tel: 01235 827720   fax: 01235 400454
e-mail: uk.orders@bookpoint.co.uk

Lines are open 9.00 a.m.–5.00 p.m., Monday to Saturday, with a
24-hour message answering service. You can also order through
the Philip Allan Updates website: www.philipallan.co.uk

© Philip Allan Updates 2004

ISBN 978-0-86003-967-9

Illustrations by James Osborne

Printed in Spain

Philip Allan Updates' policy is to use papers that
are natural, renewable and recyclable products and
made from wood grown in sustainable forests. The
logging and manufacturing processes are expected
to conform to the environmental regulations of the
country of origin.